OUT OF THE GROUND

Published by Gunpowder Press
David Starkey, Editor
PO Box 60035
Santa Barbara, CA 93160-0035

Cover photo by Greg Trainor, used by permission.

ISBN-13: 978-1-957062-10-5

www.gunpowderpress.com

Out of the Ground

Poems Inspired by
Santa Barbara Botanic Garden

Edited by
David Starkey & Chryss Yost

Gunpowder Press • Santa Barbara
2024

Celebrating the
Santa Barbara Botanic Garden

Contents

WILDS

EPILOGUE

FOREWORD

Scot Pipkin, Director of Education & Engagement
Santa Barbara Botanic Garden

Gardeners straddle two worlds. One foot is placed firmly on the solid ground of science. Obedience to biological and ecological principles is mandatory. The other foot floats in an ethereal space. Here, the senses take primacy. Beauty and delight guide the way to harmony in colors, smells, and textures. I'd argue that poetry is what unifies the gardener's work. Whether through the application of elegant theories to ensure beds full of diversity, or clever interplay of light and shadow, a garden requires poetic sensibility to have impact.

As a garden dedicated to the display and conservation of California's native plants, Santa Barbara Botanic Garden celebrates the poetry of our flora on a daily basis. The germination of a rare seed, the view from the meadow to Arlington Peak, and the careful placement of a plant whose fleeting flowers greet the visitor in just the right way—these are all manifestations of our poetic exercise.

In this volume, readers might detect a feedback loop, where the poetry of a garden inspires the written word. Some of the poems may be inspired by plants that have not been cultivated, but instead, grow wild in our hills. Here, like the gardener, the poet straddles the realms of keen observation and metaphor, using both to communicate something essential. In either case, we hope these works plant a garden in your mind and inspire you to tend the earth with ever greater care and respect.

Introduction

David Starkey, Publisher & Co-editor
Gunpowder Press

Like many local institutions, Santa Barbara Botanic Garden is beloved by generations of citizens and visitors, and yet there is something about the Garden that, even by our city's world-class standards, makes it extraordinary.

For me, part of the magic is simply arriving. As you turn off Foothill Road and begin ascending Mission Canyon, the houses fade away from the pavement, while the oak trees arch their magnificent branches over the road. When you pull into the Garden's long narrow parking lot, you sense you've entered another world.

Of course, Santa Barbara Botanic Garden is deeply rooted in *this* world—floods and fires have touched it, just as they have the rest of the city—but the way the Garden so thoroughly merges with the surrounding landscape means that, like the watershed on which it rests, it feels permanent, always a home.

Santa Barbara Botanic Garden is dedicated to the preservation and study of native plants from across California, and a ramble through the Garden can feel like a mini-tour of the Golden State. The walker is accompanied by the chitter-chatter of birds—towhees and bushtits, juncos and warblers—and the mingled scents of a dozen plants. One minute you are in the Desert, then it's the Arroyo and the Redwoods and of course the Great Meadow, where the sky always seems especially open, and the Santa Ynez Mountains, punctuated by Arlington Peak, rise in the near distance.

While the Garden is a place of wonder and joy, it is also a center of education. Children of all ages embrace hands-on learning about the natural world, especially in the Backcountry with its dedication to play and discovery. The Pritzlaff Conservation Center, which looks out on the ocean to the south, frequently hosts lectures, as well as music and poetry. And while much of Santa Barbara Botanic Garden is wild, even a short stroll through the grounds is informative. Most of us can't resist the urge to bend down and read the names of particular species—the California barrel cactus and the banana yucca, wild ginger and coyote mint, the stream orchid and the coastal woodfern. These names are themselves little poems, making a collaboration between Santa Barbara Botanic Garden and its fans in the poetry community feel almost inevitable.

Indeed, soon after I began working with Jaime Eschette, Scot Pipkin and Steve Windhager to bring more poetry to the Garden, my co-editor Chryss Yost and I put out a call for poems from poets living in Santa Barbara, San Luis Obispo, Kern, and Ventura counties. We asked for poems that aligned with Santa Barbara Botanic Garden's vision of the interdependency of plants and people. The quality of the poetry would be paramount—that went almost without saying—so we encouraged creative responses to our theme. To make the anthology as fresh as possible, we asked for poems that were previously unpublished, although we made an exception for a handful of poems that had previously appeared in the Garden's semiannual publication, *Ironwood*.

What you hold in your hands is the result of that call for poems, a panoply of verse that touches on everything from visits to the Garden to reflections on the larger California landscape to celebrations of specific plants. The book's title is drawn from Genesis 2:9: "And out of the ground made the Lord God to grow every tree that is pleasant to the sight, and good for food; the tree of life also in the midst of the garden, and the tree of knowledge of good and evil." While a few of the poets may have had religious experiences in the Garden, most of the spiritualty of the work is of a more general nature. Indeed, Chryss and I liked the openness of the phrase "out of the ground" because it echoes the wide-ranging and inclusive tone of so many of these poems.

We hope this collaboration between Santa Barbara Botanic Garden and Gunpowder Press will be a book you enjoy anywhere, but we especially like to think of readers relishing the poetry while resting on a bench beneath the towering redwoods, or crouching on one of the great sandstone boulders in the midst of fast-flowing Mission Creek, or simply sitting beneath the old live oak near the Garden's entrance, looking out on the Great Meadow in spring, the California poppies blooming like a field of golden stars.

BLOOMS

May in the Botanic Garden

I don't know what to call you,
but your lavender trumpets
call to me, clustered effusions
of silent sound, fragrant
to the listening ear.

*

Water from a boulder flows
beneath new leaves of sycamore,
spring-green hands of blessing
over what keeps coming our way.

*

Labyrinthine curl of stone,
your center is a giant comma
that tails and tails and tails
to the outermost edge of the galaxy.

*

Redwood twins, joined at the root,
you are a bit taller than
my three-year-old grandsons.
But you like to wave your arms,
like them, and touch the sky.

*

Blue-eyed grass, your little petals
near the ground are as open
as open can be, inviting us
to come on in, the pollen is fine!

*

Bracts of yellow fungus
on a chest-high stump.
Amber velvet, it would seem,
the classiness of our decay.

*

Sage at my feet, pale purple
of rising crowns, one on top of the next
in a royal line of succession.
Across the field, orange poppies
shout from a distance,
crowds at the coronation.

*

Notable penstemon, says the sign.
But aren't they all?
Yet you may be taller than the rest.
And your pink, cavernous lips and throats—
no telling what noble fare you feast upon.

*

Ghost in a pot, are you alive?
Your gray-branched stems
look like the reach of the newly dead
from a restless grave.

*

Writhing arms of manzanita,
what puts you in pain today?
Do you feel the sufferings
of this world? Because
we still eat your little apples.

The Path

The path around the meadow rewards
close attention: the wee rosettes
of the Catalina Island live-forever,
tiny yellow blooms of the saffron
buckwheat, and the noiseless ringing
of the inconspicuous canyon coral bells.

One experience links to the next:
fingertips that stroke the thready texture
of the juniper's bark are soon pricked
by the needle point leaf-tips
of Our Lord's Candle. And scooped
from the ground, the tough little leaves
of the leather oak rustle in one's palm.

Summer red berries of the summer-holly,
pale green leaves of the white sage.
Even poison oak is allowed to thrive
here where everything depends
on everything else. Stand at the southern
edge, gazing toward the mountains.
Don't those California poppies dotting
the meadow look like flecks of gold
scattered in a Sierra stream? If you could,
wouldn't you bend down and gather them?

All in a Garden Green

Venus Maidenhair Fern
Adiantum-capillus-veneris

Fronds unfurled,
                    it bears the beauty
of Venus's hair,
                        All flow and fall, the fern arches from
seeps in desert cliffs   sprawls along shady river beds, spreads

                    naked, underground.

Difficult.   Unreliable in winter.

*

Purple Needlegrass
Stipa pulchra

A California native

            almost forgotten   choked out

her nodding   flowers

        turn purple

        form needle-sharp seeds—

very easy in the right place   one unshaded

by invasives.

*

Canyon Snow Iris
Iris douglasiana
Introduced in 1975 by the Santa Barbara Botanic Garden

Its leaves enter spring like swords, slice

into light from between stones.

It performs. Wins awards. Boasts

and self-sows, shows white petals

tongued with bright yellow. It's brilliant,

handsome, and every part—

adorned with poison.

A California Superbloom

The skies have cried a hundred times,
drenching the blanket of soil below,
but the stormy weather and wet of winter
have allowed thousands of flowers to grow.
The floods have come and gone away,
banishing a decade of drought.
Blossoms burst from the earth
as nature returns and survival sprouts.
Rising up after April showers,
dancing in the breezy spring,
butterflies and bees fly petal to petal
while the birds feast and joyously sing.
The mountain air is rich in pollen
and the sweet earthy scent of sage,
poppies pry from under the rocks
as the oak trees gracefully age.
Purple irises, majestic and proud,
and opening buds of baby blue eyes,
fluttering awake after lying dormant,
look up, hopeful, toward the sky.

Earth Stars

Blue-eyed Grass - Sisyrinchium bellum

Hardy little stars
hold to dry ground,
blow in sea wind.
They hail from Inner Earth

where rock and fire give way
to a layer of cool, crepuscular sky
that clouds and clears
depending on Earth's mood.

The sky is whitish.
Stars, when they emerge,
shine blue-violet,
the most beloved color of bees.

Six-pointed Sisyrinchia
do not fall from that inner sky
but rise to Earth's crust one by one
to color the ground.

Each star lifts its tiny fire
to scout-bees who set forth
in the Sun's day of grace
and fly low over the grass

seeking blue, keenly seeking
a prize for She who stretches
in the long dawn we call
The Quickening.

At eventide, as pale lights
startle overhead, the Earth stars
fold their points and say good night.

Peonies

Last of the peonies
says the cashier
and I walk the busy street
with my strawberries and blossoms
knowing I hold poetry in my hands

Wildflower Hike

We have come to see the superbloom
painting the hillsides a vibrant yellow
in broad brushstrokes of wildflowers
emerging after the winter rains.

We are awed by mountainsides
stippled with orange poppies and purple lupines,
but the naturalist guide prefers to look up close
examining a single blue dick flower
teetering on the top of its fragile leafless stem
reaching for sunshine amidst the tall grass.

He knows these plants intimately,
draws us in close to see the elegant curve
at the top of a golden fiddleneck
swaying above tiny purple stars of fiesta flower petals.
We taste miner's lettuce fresh and pure on our tongues.

He tells us valley oaks rely on wind to propagate
through tiny petalless flowers on the tips of branches.
We linger over silver-green lace lichen
adorning the trees like tattered veils,
growing here only because the air is clean.

The wildflowers will be gone in a month.
Soon after, the grassy hills will dry to a canvas of golden brown
dotted with dark trunks and deep green leaves,
waiting out the hot summer days
for winter rains to come again.

Echeveria

Don't think your budding
                ripeness
has gone unnoticed.
In the span
         of one season,
I've watched you
              develop
from a wall flower
resting in the cool shade
      to an eye turner
taking in the full praise
              of the sun.

Your flouncy skirts
             are the envy
of all the other
              succulents.
Layers of ruffled
soft mint and smoky purple petals
        spread out over
the earthen floor.
      Bright coral blossoms
complement your gown
like elegant gloves showcasing
         long, slender arms.

   Beauty of spring
bursting forth,
          belle of the ball.

Ode to a Bush Poppy

A shout of yellow
      bush poppy singing with blooms
bright beside a sandstone boulder
      blossoms gleaming sunflares

tenacious lover of burned ground
      steep slopes seamed by sun
flaunting flowers in this garden
      a breeze plumes the green

wands tap the rock's orange lichen
      petals jitter poppy bounty
the season-carrying winds
      birds bugs bees

Spring Breezes into the Botanica

I imagine I escape from the path
tumble into the orange and green
roll wild in the silver
grasses rippling thick
pluck buckhorn blue
lie on my back in Shirley's carpet
of black sage
wind scuds the clouds
I taste spring
listen to Mission Creek
rush the canyon

Thalictrum (Meadow Rue)

In late March, it is easy
To be smitten with a sea of golden satin
Enchanted by sprays of blue
Or intoxicated
Like a bee
By the rich smell of nectar
There is no shortage of delight in these parts
But surprise requires more curiosity
Atop the fractal leaves of meadow rue
Anthers dangle like earrings, laden with promise
They wait for a gust of wind to catapult pollen grains into the skies.
Stalwart voyagers in search of their birthright.

Baby Blue Eyes Has Her Say

Nemophilia menziesii

I watch you bend low,
          despite a back that catches, to check
                              what's up.

Near hidden, we happily wander
          betwixt & between spikes of coral aloe blossoms
                    and fiddlenecks rising in multitude,

their golden heads curled
          near swallowing the hillsides,
                              drowning eager poppies
past winter's drench.

          You hear me whisper *come closer* & sweep aside
the hands of Elk Blue Rush
                    to kneel as if in prayer

for I am the flower of peace, the infinite.
          No need to fret your diminishment.
                    Grounded, we stand firm, spread willfully

blue & constant as the ever-after sky.

Deluge

When the words fall in showers
so do the names for local lupine,
what with silver also known as
evergreen or white-leaf bush, sky
also called field or Douglas annual
or dwarf, and then succulent—as if
that wasn't elegant enough—goes
by hollowleaf annual or arroyo.

Not that the plants care what we
call them, as we point in amazement
at the purpled shafts of blooms
suggesting the ecstasy of dusk drunk
in a nostalgia for just lost daylight,
burnishing all the unsaid reasons
royals robed themselves in serious
violet since Persia's Cyrus the Great.

Spring is an empire inviolate, lupine
thousands of purple pennants over
every foothill and coastal range we
somehow don't clumsily tread, but
we can't help ourselves, can we,
booting over beauty as if every-
thing belongs to us, just as if.

BRANCHES

Bird Drawn Events

The sky turned the color of rain long before the rain, pulling time together in clouds, a flight path of crows, weighted down by mouth gifts, black against the shy sky, what force have we yet to discover, the poles are wandering in search of, allow yourself only but all the resources you need, to respect the rate at which the lichen grows, nutrient air transmuted to color, falling to the base of oaks, an offering, absorb my neon velvet powder amulet, to tend the land with words that will travel into a new epoch, the joy of now, how happy we were to see the phoebe on the branch before school.

Hand-Kites

California Sycamore - Platanus racemosa

Those big white trees by the creek
drop hand-kites that spiral and sail
big as bear mud, graceful
as mourning cloak.
Even though they're magic,
she crushes them in the road
ere they fly again—pouncing,
laughing when they crunch.
Sacrificed to the boot of a child,
their bright rust flows to the foot
of a near mountain.

Likely Stories

Sycamore seedling in the creek bed,
    you are not hoping for drought,
but a flood will take you
    where you do not wish to go.
          *

Pair of oak sprouts,
    inches high,
which one of you
    will be left in shade?
          *

Slender stalk of eucalyptus,
    growing upward into light,
gravity may topple you
    before you reach your piece of sky.

Touch of Wildness

Santa Barbara Botanic Garden, March 2023

A blue day after the rains crisp
and breezy   the meadow aglow in orange
and gold poppies   a brush
                              of pink yarrow
begs to be admired.

I am drawn elsewhere—
                    to solitude
at the path's end   where the rain-sated creek
spools over scoured stone   churns
              between moss-bright boulders.
Tangles of broken branches mark
                        the water's recent flood
An untamed place where
        sycamore, oak and laurel stand sentry.

A narrow trail beckons   winds up
the steep canyon   tunnels through chaparral
                        scrub oak and manzanita.
The air tastes spring green.
        Lichen sponged rocks flank the way
and always from down below the creek's growl.

I meet no one—
                remember another botanic garden
six thousand miles away   a city garden
manicured   paved paths
                        and tropical green houses
but beautiful too   and there at a dance
                    my parents met   fell in love
and I became a glimmer on the horizon.

Ode to *Erythrina coralloides*

Coral tree, you brightly blush without
embarrassment, April your season
to go full with flowers but only that,
the greening of your leaves months away.

Nature is so single-minded about sex.
Hummingbirds and bees rush in to
the scarlet draw of the drape of your flowers,
leaving you sticky with pollen and future.

And when the blossoms from your clusters
like pinecones fall, your kernel of seed, hard
enough to pass through rats' digestive tracts,
waits to grow or poison, whichever the world wants.

The best poem about a tree

Comes not from the great geriatric mutterings on pomegranates
Nor from psalms so holy and carnal
That prayer and poem become one
Prophet and poet subsumed, consumed

Nor does it come from the Romantics with their ecstasies
Languishing for the sun
Clutched by hedonism's shuddering hand
On park benches, in fields, and yes
Under those great lyrical oaks and pines

Indeed, the best poem about a tree
(Perhaps the only poem, only tree)
Is the one above us, providing a shade so tranquil and euphoric
As to leave us no choice but to exalt its here and now

A California Coup

From the oaks grew the Pass of the Oaks,
el Paso de Robles, still growing oaks
still growing. In this town's heart,
thick oaks poke from the big
square park. The clearing appears

to have grown around the oaks still
growing, infrastructure accommodating
quercus, a phenomenon found all over
town—concrete, wires, cars,
                        swerving around still
oaks still growing, rough grey bark
so close you can almost hear it rasp.

A neat flat plot, the park is the town's
square core crayoned in grass-green
and pavestone-red, and anchored
by a Carnegie library set centrally
like a Christmas present. Here, people
gather for concerts and car shows,
unfolding their chairs under oaks
still growing imperceptibly, quietly,

though every autumn
            the trees let go, let loose a rampancy
of acorns and leaves,   abscission
as coup, reclaiming the square, the town
            with a   chaos
of themselves
            sacrificed
to the ground.

Oak Fall

The crew sprawls on the driveway, hardhats
for pillows, in the last of the tree shade. They
carried their siesta with them across the border
to give them stamina to work until first starlight
bringing down the last of our century old oak.
Landmark and shelter it had kept us

under its canopy until its new leaves didn't open
at its distant edges, dying month by month inward
to the core until done with its ring by ring autobiography.
One man commands because he risks the most
dangling high up in a web of knotted ropes
he wields a chainsaw and finds the tree's seams

with seeming ease. He ropes each chunk of branch
for the men on the ground to lower, haul, and load
into the grinder that howls the ancient song of dust to dust.
Balanced on the massive branches he undoes a century
of implacable growth, the genius of the oak—to build
upward and outward across the low sky,

turning tons of air and earth into upthrust
as if massive stone, infused with mind and pleasure
climbed to gain a portion of the sun's splendor.
Now the undoing—by noon—a skeleton, by three
—a trunk, by six—a stump. Buddhists and Jews
believe the soul needs a week to give up

the body and move on so it should be visited
and blessed those days. We might have let
the oak stand a year or two but for fear of wildfire.
By night the men are paid and gone. The house
unbuffered now is colder in the wind and we
vacuum sawdust blown under the doors.

Our displaced grey squirrels, bluejays,
and the longtime barn owl vanish. On the periphery
our eyes keep noting absence—Not here. Not here.

Coast Live Oak

Quercus Agrifolia from the Celtic quer (fine) and cuez (tree)

My breath catches when I see a cut stump
still resinous, sap damp
grain and stippling laid bare
growth and retreat
good years in the pale threads
the dark fibers of drought

This oak, hardy trunk
xylem and the phloem, wood and bark
leafy net to catch the solar stream
catkins that seed pollinating winds

Groves unsettled the first explorers
a haunting density in the light
gnarled limbs touching down to earth
oaken curves perfect
for a ship's bow, barrel staves
and charcoal, the good burn

Oaks' long hold on earth and us
world tree, axis mundi, sky and soil
rituals and sacrifice
praise poems and yellow ribbons

The world still turns without one tree
no loss without a fresh beginning
the future clenched in acorns

Highwater Mark

The redwoods' scent
is a salted evaporation
of history's highwater mark
at the onset of this warming,
the trees are solid and hollow,
held fast by an undertow
of regeneration, bodies
in alignment, eclipses
in season, we wait
for a sign of salvation,
the first of the day
is rose atop gray, a fluctuation,
my one true innocence,
I have broken no hearts

Live Oak Triptych

(Quercus agrifolia)

Sinuous is your middle name:
   Live Sinuous Oak.
     You've got the curves

and you've got the leaves and sky
   to prove it, leaning casually,
     as you do, on this stone wall.

*

Not long ago you lost a good
   part of your trunk to age and wind.
     Now remnant leaves hang

brown and shaggy, like the dusty
   folds of skin on an elephant
     collapsed by the trail.

*

Old live oak,
   dead but standing,
     now you are but a burnt snag—

and it is only the poison oak
   that holds you up
     in her blazing vines.

The Iceberg

White heat gives way to warm winds
Stroking tall gray pines in the backcountry blaze.
Off in the distance a giant sycamore leans
over the rushing Manzana, shades the allure
of a sandy bank, a desire to strip bare
lying your garments one by one on the face
of a large boulder. You stand boldly as in the gaze
of a lover, at ease watching tufts of bright green moss
drift along the seductive shimmer & dazzle,
light gleaming leisurely into the pool.
The shock of your nakedness
letting go slow &
easy into the
plunge.

FIELDS

Bountiful

This was the winter of reprieve—
After six years of sand in the throat,
of drowned canyon boulders emerging
at the bottom of reservoirs, ghosts taunting
us with our own mortality of dry bones—
A season too long stark,
as the curling bark from manzanita
branches among the coyote bush that held on,
sheltering quail and lending a defiant perch
for the curved notes of the California thrasher
over the chapparal, before the water returned,
in the bountiful way only California in winter
can cause sere, leonine hills crouched
waiting brown and blond —
to leap up with new grass, shading curves
peridot and emerald, even the blue green
of the sea below cliffs was borrowed,
as water married earth, and woke seeds
that had slept years, before bringing forth
chalices of gold California poppies,
blue and white lupine spears
saying amen to the cloudbursts.

An Island Reveals

—after the music of Cody Westheimer

The grass grows green
with the heavy rain
of an unexpected spring

Hills thick and lush
and soon scattered over
with gold and purple blooms
beetles and spiders
swallowtails and sulphurs
hairstreaks and skippers and blues

Through February and March
the rains continue, each new shower
a welcome surprise

And then the gray dome of May
and June, the runic signals
of fog and mist
and the murky distance of mountains
at dusk and dawn

Someone should write a song
of the Western rattlesnake
and the California wild rose
the Hoaryleaf Ceanothus
and the San Andreas Fault

A song of the thousand years
twice told and the wisdom
that sprouts like chanterelles
in the leaf litter of Valley Oaks

like the springtails leaping
from old slabs of bark
and decomposing trees

The wisdom that slinks from sight
as quickly as the skink beneath your feet
there and gone in the rapid stroke
of the beak of the snowy plover
or the egret or the Clapper Rail

Someone should write a song
that only listens

For the rains will cease
and the sky dry to a milky blue

The sere fields of grass will bend
to the Santa Ana Winds
and a spark may catch and blaze
through the summer
the autumn, the arid winter
It may all burn to smoky ash

Or our luck may hold
the chaparral retain its scent
of sage and coyote brush
the wind do nothing more
than ruffle the yellow
petals of the monkeyflower
We may come to wisdom gradually
the way an island seen from across
an expanse of ocean slowly reveals
its spine as afternoon
and then evening come on

greener grass

silver snail tracks
      glisten on sidewalks

black cows on the hill
      hidden in yellow wildflowers

plenty of fresh grass
      to choose from after all the rain

but they scurry up to the ridge line
      where the view is no doubt better

and here's the thing—the life I want
      is the one I have

Mission Creek

I am lying on wet sandstone,
looking at the oak trees
and the hazy, shredded blue.

Above me are telephone lines,
nine lines, I counted because
the sun is warm on my forehead.
Because my feet are cool near the creek.

And because there is this rush,
a heavy loud rush,
beside me
beneath me
behind me.

And I am thinking, this is happening
even when I am not here
but when I am, I really am.

Solace

Gold
poppies
spring to life.
Bold, neon splashes
gild hills and meadows,
gladden eyes and heal hearts,
soothe troubled, turbulent minds
with orange glow and vibrancy flow.
No place for sorrow or grieving now
this gold unfolds promise of solace.

Landscapes

Fog at the brow of the mountain
Dew on leaves and grasses
Caught between mountain and the sea

The smell of earth, its own smell
The smell of water
Of fragrant blossoms

The color blue outruns the fog
Warms petals in search of light
Sparkles on dewdrops

Rough bark reminds me of elders
The trails, well-traveled by the man I called Dad
Rainbow of color everywhere, my dancing sister

I hear the Sycamore leaves, *welcome, welcome*
Deep red-brown manzanita bark, look at me
Smooth, like young niece's skin

Vulnerable to drought and storm alike
Nature's garden offers me a soft blanket
Much needed cariño, affection that encourages peace

And strength
Respite from the invented busyness of our times,
A chance to remember everything we need is given to us

This poem is not to the lone yucca, or thistle
But to the whole ecology of a landscape, the interdependence
Of an eco-system, the kind that once sustained all its inhabitants

This poem grounds us to earth
This poem pushes *I* to the side for the *we*, we depend on our community
To care about both exterior and interior landscapes

Like a Poppy

Like a poppy, I fold into myself,
Shivering against the darkness of life's cold night,
Wondering if dawn will come again.
The lonely blackness envelops me,
And my memories of sunlight grow dim,
Sometimes disappearing altogether.
I bow my head in a nearly empty hope.
The night, unimpressed, silently plods on.
And on.

Then, almost imperceptibly,
A faint light hints at the horizon of my consciousness.
I wonder if it is even there at all.
Ever so slowly, the blackness begins to yield,
And something stirs inside me,
Inviting me to find some gratitude.
In the cold, gray light, I see my circle of companions
Who have weathered the night beside me,
And I am thankful.

In our collective faith in dawn's arrival
(Some more certain than others),
We gaze together at the eastern sky.
Gray adds indigo,
Indigo adds scarlet,
Scarlet adds orange,

And soon, almost unconsciously,
I find myself opening wide to the morning's brilliance.

I recognize its impermanence.
I understand that night will fall again.
But for this moment, this glorious, liberating moment,
I am bathed in light and warmth.
That is enough.

Orange in Santa Barbara

A zealous mass of seeds growing within the depths of who I am
Sprouting orange all over the hillside, creating a mirage of poppies
The flowers dance in the wind, swaying gracefully in their own ballet
Petals of silk awaiting the gentle touch of their pollinator guests
Monarch butterflies float like clouds from one flower to the next
Showing off lacey wings of vivid tangerine and ebony
Flying into the sky the light reflects off their delicate frames
Revealing a horizon of burning fire and amber accents
A new sunset has blessed our beloved home
As another day in the gardens has come to an end

California Spring, After a Wet Winter

Like an invading army, the poppies are
occupying my yard, overwhelming other plants,
swarming over open spaces,
insinuating themselves like spies into cracks in the patio
and under the fence.
They put down their long tap roots,
deep as the trenches dug by soldiers.
All day their orange heads dominate
the landscape, reinforcements arriving daily.
At night blossoms retreat into their shells,
waiting to march forth anew in the morning.

Bee's Bliss Sage

Salvia leucophyllax

For years I've whiffed its fragrance
thrilled to dowse the house
time to time with a lit swatch
snuffing out any intrusive spirit
that may have invaded
through dream or crack, my shadow
darkening those imperial frills.

On closer look, I become one
with the bees all bumble and buzz
as they dive deep inside
the floral centers slurping nectar
getting drunk on a Sunday afternoon
oblivious to the extravagance
of poppies waving and weaving
their way through every green thing,
little voices singing *poppies poppies*
while I dine on the honey of bliss.

Dedication

A dancing canopy
of bees huddle
and hum, undeterred
by the stiff sway
of alluring lavender
spears —
intricate bent antennae
probe and prowl
as summer
blossoms abide —
lively clusters then turn
like discerning devotees
to red willow's reward,
to the purity of purple sage,
their fervor, their fragile
double wings carry
home collected nectar

Haiku

Cows graze in a field
of mustard; dark islands in
a sea of yellow.

Suns and Shadows

Bees bustle between
the dark purple primrose

and the shining orange tree,
from lofty white blossoms

destined to be miniature
suns, to violet flowers,

content to glow in shadow.
They sip the sweetness of each

At Home in a Garden

Memory dwindles but
not completely. Look.
Here is the four year old child
following her mother
around their London garden
where grew flowers from California
achillea, bachelor's buttons
blue lupins, goldenrod and
poppies, cups of gold.

Now she wanders in a California garden
fingers the sage leaves
to release their spicy scent
hears the rain-filled creek roar
spies the darting lizards
sits and writes a poem
surprised and grateful
to find herself once more
at home in a garden.

compass light

Step outside your window just
as the trapeze bar of spring arcs towards you

Delight in its irresistible invitation,
and your weightlessness
          just as you catch
sight of lion-headed mustard fields roaring
below with enthusiastic yeses

Listen, the bees tumble-whistle and yawn
the morning open

Glimpse spiders lamp-wrapping shawls
of midnight vigil

Ignore the always-crow on the roof's edge
hackling and heckling

Stay

Stay in the compass rhythm until
light tastes
like almost summer and sticks
like lemonade to your fingers

A Visit to the Botanic Garden

Wander without map, plan, or nametag,
unlike the bees who hive by a white sign:
Bees Working / Abejas Trabajando.

Out of an oval opening in a coastal oak,
an ecstasy of bees exits. Their zigzags
draw me closer and I wonder:

How brave would I have to be to put my hand in
the tree's crevice, extract hard-earned sweetness?
I mind my manners.

Last year's sting lingers as most wounds do.
I leave the honey bees to their work.
Enter the raised courtyard.

A young mother feeds her baby,
pale breast in hand, she smiles
as her older daughter frolics free.

I circle back towards the grove of Redwoods.
Renewed in the stillness of a forest bath,
a towhee's song sets the world straight.

Soon other voices join joyous:
Goldfinches, Orioles, Sparrows.
As if to say, all's well in the world today.

WILDS

Prayer to Jacaranda

You who hold the knives in light,
bare branches, empty hands lifted,
hear me. I am lost beyond wood.
Body untouched. Begin, I ask you,
with wind, and may doves appear later,
for the body needs, must be, lofted.
Whirlwind or cyclone, unstrung
or restrung. One dark spine with
its dozen fronds. A chest of bone.

Leaf out, Artemis, let chlorophyll
harvest light, let green come to
the beholder; may pleasure come,
so, in me, hungering as a vine, come
twining, turned and turning, let spin
cast its finespun through my interior
trees, violet fire up its flame, burn
as it will beyond lavender to slate.

Lament of the Yucca Bevifolia

(Joshua Tree)

My name is the sound of what you want
to spit out. Wrapped in my own dead
leaves, at night I stare into the trillion stars
and wonder if loneliness is the price
of light. We long for the same things,
but if you touch me with a naked hand
I will cut you.
              Where would I be then?

The Audience for Poetry

This evening I'm reading
my poems to the trees,
grateful for the approbation
of desiccated leaves,
for clouds that made
a few suggestions before
they wandered off,
ignoring the sky's
fading page.
         I resign
myself to whatever
presents itself with dusk,
and to what, I guess,
that usually implies....
I'm admiring the last
cymbidiums, the smoldering
light of nasturtiums, the blooming
pittosporum and—even the dark
scrawl of liquidambars
outlining our long-range
chances against a sea-
deep blue.
        Tomorrow,
I'll be here again—sitting
in the same sun-cracked
wicker chair, holding
one-sided conversations
with the garden's green,
weed-thick stanzas
making it clear that
not even the least of them
has much use for me....

Outdoor School Lessons

They taught me to trust in the wilderness,
to believe in bats and bobcats obscured
in the black of new moon nights.
They taught me the oak trees would hold me,
strong and mighty branches, tangled,
but I was safe underneath their leaves.
They taught me to value the vultures and condors,
underappreciated scavengers cleaning up carcasses,
preventing putrid pollution.
They taught me the power of plants,
to classify coyote brush and sage,
observe the delicate monarchs on milkweed.
They taught me to pray for the puma,
respect the wrath of the rattlesnake
and fight for the frogs and foxes.
They taught me the earth's crust is rich
like chocolate coating on a peanut core—
it melts away just as fast,
so savor every bit and make it last.

Prayer

—*S. K.*

I am petitioning the plants again,
the field sedge like sandstone
in afternoon light, seedheads
sorrow-knotted, thorny
        as I am.

Wildflowers die as if it's effortless
to do so. They die in the scant shade
of the chapparal. They dry out
in the meadow, crumble in the sun.
No ambitions beyond a season.

There is a time for death.
It isn't, shouldn't be, now.
How will the hollow earth hold
these redwoods and this grief
        and not collapse?

The sphinx moths swarm
the purple sage at dusk.
The monarchs are gone.
The caterpillars gone.
Gold-flecked packets
dangle from the manzanita,
growing impossible wings.

Manzanita

Of the lacquered
Branches, the healing
Leaf. Your existence
A reminder there is more
To this earth than war
Wherever it is
It is everywhere.
When I close my eyes
I can dream the last
of the blushed campanitas
You held on to
At winter's end
They live inside
Me now, persisting.

A Branch Has Come Down

A dry branch
on a bench
I pick it up.

The branch asks me questions
as I hold it above my white paper.

Its shadow enlarges
into a raptor.

Lifts me
into the blue gauze
of sky.

Burying the Whale

Gophers muddied the pool,
braids delivered Providence,
(ground gave to ground)
boring the curb a vertebrae.
At the reception, they foraged
(took) Matilija poppies for cake
while dinosaurs roared
their (Clathrus) roars.
Father toasted the heckler
(Tilikum raged like icing).
Vases collected (Petals to dirt),
Velella velellas to cow.

Here...

a desert, a diary
in granite and ash,
a rustle in the underbrush,
a scattering of light.

The Botanic Garden is the rooted
    and the winged.

Redwood, manzanita and chaparral,
it is the torn, parched and tattered,
the backlit and tangled.

Its inhabitants are nest builders,
seed scatterers, murmurations of children,
and pollinators.

An acoustic mosaic
    trilling,
      buzzing,
cooing,
        warbling,
            distant hawk screech,
  and fragments of quiet
conversation further up the path.

It is fragrant raggedy hollows
and ancient violet,
    sage and ochres.

Daily, it is both graveyard...and a nursery.

The Garden is a restless painting,
a school house...an apothecary for the weary.

If one lingers,
you may begin
to decipher
the language of roots, sparrows,
a skittering lizard,
the tender dusk,
one pale feather floating
     to the earth.

Viriditas

Minnesota-born, I'm like a stalwart
spruce or elm. But in the California
garden store, I find rows of orange
and green jewels, smooth and prickly mysteries.

They are humble plants in dusty soil,
suffused with eccentricity, as if God—
bored with shrubs and trees—carved the thumbs
of jade petals, octopus arms of aloes.

Hildegard of Bingen wrote that God
quickens the soul, as the sun inspires plants.
The One Light makes green things green, animates

the seed within. Creators all, we shape
the maple leaves or cactus spines that sprout
from us, the flesh-borne signatures of our days.

Bitter Gooseberry

Of all the gooseberries here we get the one called bitter,
scarcely worth the effort for human consumption even if
birds gobble its fruit down, camouflage under its thorny thickets.

And even in Santa Barbara where the season is merely mild,
the Ribes amarum is winter deciduous, content to join
the rest of the world in celebrating spring's coming out party.

Let's love all of nature that's not meant for us, the plain
and untasty, the hidden beneath scrub oaks in impassable hills.

There are plenty of gooseberries elsewhere for humans to enjoy,
served up in crumbles and fools, centering beloved Chekhov,
resplendent fuchsia flowering from its don't touch spines.

Then again what do I know, east coast born and analogous
to the invasive Jersey cudweed, ugly as the sneer a local
makes when snarling, "You aren't from around here, are you."

Catch

You always said you needed to
"catch yourself"
as if Monday through Friday
was an act of falling.
Falling on bad luck.
Falling on hard times.
Falling
against the grind
of daily life,
the endless electricity bills and broken toasters and email chains.

But the weekends—
they were for
catching.
For cruising to the Santa Cruz Mountains,
where city sounds
turned to blue jay trills.
You taught me how to catch myself
on redwood branches
on dappled sunlight
on creeks that cooled our toes on summer days.

Now that you're gone,
I find myself falling.
Stumbling over memories,
Tripping over too many to-dos,

Falling
prey to the hustle,
endlessly running.

You're no longer here to catch me.
It feels like free-falling to even say that simple truth aloud.

Still, you taught me—
the weekends are for
catching.
So I reach out with my ears,
my heart
my sore eyes
catching myself
on redwood branches
on dappled sunlight
on creeks that cool my toes on summer days.
Nestled, here—*right here*—
within the Botanic Garden.
Soaring *sequoia sempervirens,*
a tall haven.

They catch me
every time.

Finally, freesia

geranium
 baby's breath
  youngberry
   wild sunflower
    beach moonflower
   daydream cosmos
  star jasmine
 stargazer lily

         forget-me-not

morning glory
 nightshade
  naked ladies
   touch-me-not
    periwinkle
    sweet alyssum
   naked-man orchid
  triumph tulip
 honeysuckle

         snapdragon

opium poppy
 American wisteria
  red columbine
   bloodroot
    crocosmia lucifer
   trinity flower
  angel's trumpet
 trumpet vine

         breath of heaven

This Morning I Ate the Holes

left by tiny snails in my Tuscan kale,
wrinkled holder of holes.

I'd gone to the garden and knelt to cut
but couldn't after finding on the underside
a creature with a spiral galaxy

riding its back. I left it on the leaf,
ten-thousand-times the snail's size, where
the little alien opened portals

with its twelve-thousand teeth. Glad
it didn't end up one of my regrets.
I returned to the kitchen with some

greens, guest-free, and hoped nothing
would swoop down or crawl up to swallow
the mini designer

who offered me new world views, one
after another and proof we are not alone.

Autumn in the Garden

—*I. M. Margaret Starkey, 1929-2023*

Say it: sycamore leaves curling
in late September, the base
of the black oak already carpeted
with dun-colored leaves,
little dead clumps in the branches,
waiting to fall.
          This is the season
of hearkening, when lichen
listen for the answer to their silence,
and hear it only in the redbud's whisper,
the skittering of lizards in the duff,
the wing-thrum of a quail covey
bursting from its hiding place
then circling back into the tall grass,
sere, fading into the next life.

EPILOGUE

This Path Leaves the Garden

Part of us was here
before we were here

in the spread of oxalis,
the roots of goldenrod.

We can wonder about life's meaning
but are not smarter than

the bees hiving in the oak
the frog croaking from the creek

where water slurs into murk
under a footbridge rebuilt after fire.

We know how to tell stories,
pass them on in a kind of evolution,

but we forget, walk on, cross the bridge,
and break the spider's web.

Carmen Alexander is a poet, gardener, songwriter, photographer, artist, singer, and self-proclaimed hummingbird nerd. She spent her youth in Almena, Kansas, a town with a population of less than 500, and currently resides in Newbury Park, California, where she writes poetry and song lyrics for her country/rock band. Her poetry incorporates themes of introspection, everyday struggles, loss, empowerment, and appreciation for the small things. Her work appears in *redrosethorns magazine*, Thistle & Thorn Press, Prairie Dog Press, and carmenalexander.com.

Lori Anaya, bilingual teacher, poet, and writer, is one of five sisters. She writes across genres, picture book to adult. She is a Southcoast Writing Project Fellow, an active member of the Society of Children's Book Writers and Illustrators, and Young Writers Academy instructor. Published in the *Santa Barbara Literary Journal, Avalon Literary Review*, and la bloga.blogspot.com. When not writing, she rides a paint mare into a central coastal land preserve where nature overlooks the fact that she is human.

Sarah Blakely is a California central coast native who has been writing poetry since she could form sentences on paper. She has won awards for her writing and has been published in several small press anthologies, an international magazine, and two self-published books. She enjoys writing songs and poetry, hiking, going to music shows, researching family history, and practicing astrology. She is currently a student at the University of Oregon studying Women's and Gender studies. Find her work on Instagram at @sarahb.poetry.

Gudrun Bortman grew up in Hamburg, Germany, and moved to the US in her twenties. She is an artist, a garden designer and a poet. Her poems have been published in *Sukoon Literary Magazine, Panoply, San Pedro River Review, Miramar, Salt, Psalms of Cinder & Silt, Santa Barbara Seasons* and several anthologies published by Gunpowder Press. Her chapbook *Fireweed* was released in October 2018 by The Poetry Box. She lives in Santa Barbara, California.

Sally Anderson Boström grew up in Santa Barbara's Mission Canyon riding horses, catching tadpoles, and looking for coyote skulls. She holds a degree in Creative Writing from UC Santa Cruz, a Ph.D. in American Literature from Uppsala University, and currently splits her time between Santa Barbara and Stockholm. Her poetry has appeared in numerous American and European journals. Her first chapbook, *Harvest*, was published by Kelsay Books in 2021. www.sallyandersonbostrom.com.

M. L. Brown is the author of *Call It Mist*, winner of the Three Mile Harbor Press Book Prize. She is also the author of *Drought*, winner of the Claudia Emerson Chapbook award. Her work has appeared in *Valparaiso Poetry Review, Prairie Schooner*, and *Cave Wall* among other journals and anthologies.

Christopher Buckley is editor of *Naming the Lost: The Fresno Poets—Interviews & Essays* (Stephen F. Austin State Univ. Press, 2021). His most recent book of poetry is *One Sky to the Next*, winner of the Longleaf Press Book Prize.

Carolyn Chilton Casas is a Reiki master and teacher who writes about nature, mindfulness, and ways to heal. Her articles and poems have appeared in *Braided Way, Energy, Odyssey, Grateful Living, Reiki News Magazine*, and in other publications. Read more of Carolyn's work on Facebook, on Instagram @mindfulpoet_, or in her first collection of poems titled *Our Shared Breath*.

Clayton Clark is a painter and poet. Her work has appeared in *Juxtapose, SALT* and the anthology *While You Wait* among other places. She came to poetry late in life and is grateful for the world it has opened.

Fran Davis has been a Sierra Club member for 35 years and is a lifelong lover of earth's botanical garden. A journalist who writes for *Coastal View News*, she has had poetry, stories and essays published in *Passager, Calyx*, the *Chattahoochee Review, Askew, The Hopper* from Green Writers Press, several Gunpowder Press anthologies and others. She is the winner of the Lamar York Prize for Nonfiction and a Pushcart Press nominee.

Marsha de la O is a lecturer in at California State University, Channel Islands, where she teaches poetry and creative writing. Her latest book, *Creature*, is forthcoming from Pitt Poetry Series. She is the author of *Every Ravening Thing, Antidote for Night*, and *Black Hope*. Her poems have appeared in *The New Yorker, The Slowdown*, and many other journals, and she is a recipient of the Morton Marcus Poetry Prize. She and her husband are founders of the Ventura County Poetry Project.

Kurt Duran is an east coast transplant living in Santa Barbara with his husband, their Maltipoo, and two chickens.

Ana Ellickson writes about fierce girls, family curses, and everyday magic. Her debut novel *The Vanishing Station* is forthcoming from Abrams/Amulet Books. Ever searching for stories, she has hiked over 500 miles across Spain, explored elephant sanctuaries in Chiang Mai, and taught English in Prague. She loves to wander the trails in the Santa Barbara Botanic Garden with her boyfriend and their two furry goldies.

Kimbrough Ernest resides in Ventura County and teaches poetry to elementary school students through California Poets in the Schools.

Mary Freericks has an M.F.A. in poetry from Columbia University. She has five poetry memoirs beginning with *Blue Watermelon* and ending with *Swimming Through the Generations*. Her latest book is *Inventions*. She is now working on *Avalanche from Widow to Single*. She taught for Californian Poets in the Schools and the N.J. State Council on the Arts. Her prize-winning poems have been widely published.

Cie Gumucio is a writer, artist, and Poet/Teacher with Cal Poets in the Schools. In 2021, Cie worked with the Santa Barbara Museum of Art and Botanic Garden to help the monarch butterflies; "Poetry with Wings" engaged over 1000 students and won a Santa Barbara Beautiful Award. Her solo art exhibit is "Writers in Search of the Sacred." She curated the TEDx "Rediscovery of the Senses." Her writing and performance was selected for Speaking of Stories and her poetry is published in several anthologies.

Hannah Huff is a poet from Paso Robles, California (The Pass of the Oaks aka Where Quercus Caucus). She holds a BA in English from UC Los Angeles and an MFA in Creative Writing from CSU Long Beach. Her writing has appeared in publications such as *The Nasiona, Terrain.org, The Portland Review*, and *The Coil Magazine*.

Kristin Kane is a twenty-two year old woman from Santa Barbara. She has a passion for poetry that began during her elementary school years when she won her first contest. She attends Antioch University as a human development and psychology major who hopes to pursue a career as a licensed therapist in her future. Kristin enjoys horseback riding, listening to music, going to the beach and spending quality time with loved ones in her free time.

Peggy Kelly is a retired high school English teacher and a fellow of the South Coast Writing Project. She spends time each summer guiding beginning educators in how to use writing in their classrooms and in their lives. Her essays on teaching and writing have been published in *California English*.

Isabelle Kim-Sherman is an eighteen-year-old from Santa Barbara, California. Her work has been published by *Tablet Magazine* as well the Jane Austen Society of North America. She has attended the California State Summer School for the Arts with a focus on creative writing and the Iowa Young Writers' Studio with a focus on TV writing. She is an undergraduate student at Yale University, class of 2027.

Gabriella Klein's first book, *Land Sparing*, was published by Nightboat Books in 2015 as winner of the Nightboat Poetry Prize. *Land Sparing* was also nominated for the California Book Award in 2016. She received her MFA in Poetry from Vermont College.

Perie Longo, Santa Barbara Poet Laureate (2007-09) has published four books of poetry which include *Milking the Earth* (1986), *The Privacy of Wind* (1997), *With Nothing behind but Sky: a journey through grief* (2006), and *Baggage Claim* (2014) Individual poems appear in *Atlanta Review, International Poetry Review, Miramar, Nimrod, Passage,Paterson Literary Review, Prairie Schooner, Rattle, Salt, Solo Novo*, and others. She is on the staff of the Santa Barbara Writer's Conference and teaches privately. On the Board of the Nuclear Age Peace Foundation, in 2005 she was invited to Kuwait University to speak about "Poetry as a Way to Peace".

Jasmine Marshall Armstrong is a native of Santa Barbara, raised in San Luis Obispo County. Her work has appeared in *The Dewdrop, Cathexis Northwest Press, Typishly, America Magazine, Sojourners Magazine, Poets Reading the News, In Parenthesis* and numerous literary anthologies. She divides her time between the Central Valley and Grover Beach, California. She has an MFA from Fresno State University and an MA in Humanities from the University of California.

Juliane McAdam is a California native who grew up in the stark beauty of the Mojave Desert. She spent the last 27 years of a 40-year teaching career teaching English and Spanish to middle school students in Los Angeles, writing poems with them. Now retired and living near Morro Bay on California's beautiful Central Coast, she enjoys walks, kayaking, playing piano, and writing poems to record observations and memories.

Anita McLaughlin works at Blanchard Community library and lives in Santa Paula on the edge of the Santa Clara River. She writes about wildlife in Heritage Valley within the shadow of South Mountain. Her poems have been published in *SMC Emeritus Chronicles, Askew, Canyon Chronicle* and the VCWC anthology, *Nuance*.

Anne Neubauer is a local poet who has resided in Santa Barbara for over 30 years. Her poetry is inspired by nature, and the proximity of her home to the Santa Barbara Botanic Gardens affords her many evening walks throughout its quiet gardens and grounds.

Enid Osborn served as Poet Laureate of Santa Barbara (2017-2019). Her book *When the Big Wind Comes* (2015, BIG YES Press) takes place in Southeast New Mexico, where her family raised quarter horses. Her themed chapbooks include *Wormlore, Pedregosa Street, Queen in Exile, Milagro*, and—forthcoming—*Little Wakes*. Her poem "The Place of Loss" was nominated by *Askew* for a Pushcart Prize. In 2011, she co-edited the anthology *A Bird Black as the Sun / California Poets on Crows & Ravens*.

Melinda Palacio is the current Poet Laureate of Santa Barbara. Her poetry collections include *Folsom Lockdown*; *How Fire Is a Story, Waiting*; and *Bird Forgiveness*.

Scot Pipkin is a naturalist who hopes to make the wonder and mystery of the world around him more tangible through poetry.

Susan Shields was introduced to poetry in three languages while in high school in England. Reading and writing poetry has helped her celebrate and survive many stages of her life and continues to inspire her every day.

George HS Singer's work has appeared in *Cumberland Poetry Review, Hampden-Sydney Review, The Massachusetts Review, Prairie Schooner, Tar River Poetry*, and the poetry collection *Rare Feathers: Poems on Birds & Art*. His poetry collection, *Ergon*, was published by WordTech. He has attended several poetry festivals and poetry seminars at the Frost Place, New Hampshire, and studied with Molly Peacock and Patrick Donnelly. Singer was a Zen Buddhist priest before earning his PhD in special education from the University of Oregon. He recently retired as a professor at UC Santa Barbara.

David Starkey served as Santa Barbara's 2009-2011 Poet Laureate. The Founding Director of the Creative Writing Program at Santa Barbara City College, he is currently Co-editor of *Anacapa Review* and *The California Review of Books*, and Publisher and Co-editor of Gunpowder Press. His most recent book is *Cutting It Loose*. He frequently collaborates with Santa Barbara Botanic Garden.

Daniel Thomas's second poetry book, *Leaving the Base Camp at Dawn*, was published in 2022. His first collection, *Deep Pockets*, won a 2018 Catholic Press Award. He has published poems in many journals, including *Southern Poetry Review, Nimrod, Poetry Ireland Review, The Bitter Oleander, Atlanta Review*, and others. He has an MFA in poetry from Seattle Pacific University, as well as an MA in film and a BA in literature. danielthomaspoetry.com

Emma Trelles is the 9th Poet Laureate of Santa Barbara (2021-23) and the author of *Tropicalia* (U. of Notre Dame), winner of the Andrés Montoya Poetry Prize. She's received writing fellowships from the California Arts Council, the Academy of American Poets, CantoMundo, and the Florida Division of Cultural Affairs. She curates the Mission Poetry Series and edits the Alta California Chapbook Series, bilingual editions published by Gunpowder Press.

Jace Ryan Turner is a librarian at the Santa Barbara Public Library. He also likes to write poems, some of which have appeared in *While You Wait: A Collection by Santa Barbara County Poets* (Gunpowder Press, 2021) and *SALT*.

Isabelle Walker is a longtime Santa Barbara resident, writer, and teacher. She writes about art, architecture and the natural world for magazines and newspapers. Her poems have appeared in *December, The Maine Review, The Sierra Nevada Review, While You Wait*, and the *Santa Barbara Literary Journal*.

Joseph Warren is native Californian who has lived in Ventura since 2008. The natural beauty of the Central Coast has provided him with solace and inspiration for more than 60 years. Retired from a career in public relations and corporate communications, he is now able to write purely for pleasure, which he considers a wondrous gift.

Norma Wightman lives in Morro Bay, California, where she walks the beach daily, leads nature hikes in local state parks and enjoys yoga, kayaking and birding around the beautiful central coast. Norma has published chapbooks for family and friends and her poems have appeared in online journals, local publications and art exhibits.

Paul Willis has published seven collections of poetry, the most recent of which is *Somewhere to Follow* (Slant Books, 2021). Individual poems have appeared in *Poetry, Christian Century, Writer's Almanac*, and the *Best American Poetry* series. He is a former poet laureate for the city of Santa Barbara and has served as an artist-in-residence in North Cascades National Park.

George Yatchisin is the author of *Feast Days* (Flutter Press, 2016) and *The First Night We Thought the World Would End* (Brandenburg Press, 2019). His poems have been published in journals including *Antioch Review, Askew*, and *Zocalo Public Square*. He is co-editor of the anthology *Rare Feathers: Poems on Birds & Art* (Gunpowder Press, 2015), and his poetry appears in anthologies including *Reel Verse: Poems About the Movies* (Everyman's Library 2019).

Chryss Yost is a poet, designer, and educator based in Santa Barbara. She is the co-editor of Gunpowder Press and served as Santa Barbara Poet Laureate from 2013-2015. She was selected by Patricia Smith for the Patricia Dobler Poetry Prize.

GUNPOWDER PRESS
SHORELINE VOICES SERIES

2021
While You Wait:
Poems by Santa Barbara County Poets
Edited by Laure-Anne Bosselaar
Available in print and online at WhileYouWait.org

2021
Big Enough for Words: Poems & Vintage Photographs
from California's Central Coast
Edited by David Starkey, George Yatchisin and Chryss Yost
Available online at BigEnoughforWords.com

2017
To Give Live a Shape:
Poems Inspired by the Santa Barbara Museum of Art
Edited by Davud Starkey and Chryss Yost

2016
What Breathes Us:
Santa Barbara Poets Laureate 2005-2015
Edited by Davud Starkey

2015
Rare Feathers: Poems on Birds & Art
Edited by Nancy Gifford, Chryss Yost, and George Yatchisin

2014
Buzz: Poets Respond to SWARM
Edited by Nancy Gifford and Chryss Yost

www.ingramcontent.com/pod-product-compliance
Lightning Source LLC
Chambersburg PA
CBHW031449120626
46545CB00006B/2617